The Dwelling Place

Bishop George C. Searight

Foreword by Bishop Donald Hilliard, II

THE DWELLING PLACE

Published by GEMS

For information:

GEMS, A Publishing Company

P.O. Box 21

Franklin Park, NJ 08823

ISBN: 0-9793856-0-1

Photography by Darnell Gourdine

Cover Design by Miller Graphics

Printed in the United States of America

"Bishop George Searight has done it again. Not only does he captivate your mind through the preached Word, but as a writer he captivates your heart as he illustrates the complete essence of worship. The dynamics of worship is revealed and made relevant to any process a believer may be experiencing. I never knew how important my worship was to God until reading ***The Dwelling Place****. I now understand that every situation God allowed me to experience, birthed major worship in me that brought me closer to Him.* ***The Dwelling Place*** *is not only for Praise and Worship Leaders, but for anyone who has the heart of worship at the forefront of his or her life. I must say that this book is a must have for every Kingdom-minded believer. It will definitely realign your mind with the mind of God for all who dare to dwell in* ***The Dwelling Place****."*

Hezekiah Walker, Senior Pastor
Love Fellowship Tabernacle, Brooklyn, New York

*"****The Dwelling Place*** *is a refreshing look at the actions, protocols and demonstrations of what we call Praise and Worship –Bishop Searight reaches beyond going through the motions into captivating real worship and praise. He has written and made a literary reality available to not only the church but to any individual who seeks to enter into the presence of God through Praise and Worship.*

I have known Bishop Searight from his youth; Praise and Worship has always emanated from every fiber of his being. This is a world changing book that has the capacity to elevate the way in which the church understands Praise and Worship. Bishop Searight's writing serves as an unveiling of true Praise and Worship and it could not have come at a timelier period in the world of Christendom."

Evangelist Shirley (Mom) Graham
Holy Temple Church of God and Christ, Toms River, N.J.

"Bishop George Searight has done it!! The Dwelling Place is an awesome book that challenges today's churchgoers to deepen their passion and to aggressively pursue the presence of God. As I read the book, I found myself wanting to know Jesus Christ better. I appreciate Bishop Searight's sensitivity to the Holy Spirit and his unrelenting commitment to worship. This is a must read!"

John E. Guns, Senior Pastor
Saint Paul Church, Inc., Jacksonville, Florida

I would like to dedicate
this book to my parents,
Thomas and Senobia Searight

ACKNOWLEDGEMENTS

I WANT TO THANK MY wife, Mary. Thank you for allowing me to be me. To my children, Erika and George, thank you for the inspiration that you've given me to finish this book. And to my siblings, Diane, Thomas and Bill, thank you for your support.

Thank you to my Abundant Life Church family. To my Elders, Ministers, Ministers in Training, Deacons, Deacons in Training, and Trustees, thank you for your continual prayers and support. To the Sanctuary Ministries—Teya (Worship Team), Choir, Musicians, Ushers, Greeters, Media Team and Security—thank you for embracing this incredible call to worship.

Bishop Donald Hilliard, II, my spiritual father, thank you for your continual encouragement, prayers and support. I would also like to thank every man and woman of God who allowed me to release my gift and calling in the earth.

Finally, I want to thank everyone who took the time to read the manuscript. To my editors, Sarah Bobien, Christian Johnson, Tracy Uzell and Taydra Mitchell-Jackson thank you for your time and expertise. Thank you Dwayne and Danielle Jennings for believing in me and making this dream come true. (I could not have done it without you.)

CONTENTS

FOREWORD

"IS THERE A DAVID in the house?" This is a common phrase resounding from the Abundant Life Family Worship Church (where Bishop George Searight is the founder and Senior Pastor), a growing, vibrant and thriving community of faith whose foundation has been firmly laid with praise and worship at its core.

Bishop Searight is no stranger to praise and worship, having served as a praise & worship leader on the evangelistic circuit for many years. Prior to becoming the Assistant to the Pastor and the head praise and worship Leader at the historic Second Baptist Church, now Cathedral International Church in Perth Amboy, New Jersey, he assisted in moving the church further into the power of Pentecostal praise. His teaching, preaching and song writing all reflect first a deep love and admiration for the Lord Jesus Christ; secondly, a burning desire for the people of God to "catch it" and that they would become true worshippers. For the Lord indeed desires that we worship Him and that we worship Him in spirit and in truth.

Nurtured in the Church of God In Christ in his early life and the revival movement, his ministry now is inclusive of not only Pentecostal and charismatic worship and praise, but a growing appreciation of liturgical "high church worship". It is rare that one finds an individual with the tenacity and energy of Bishop Searight. We celebrate this, his first publication and believe that it will be a powerful starting point of other writings to come.

We commend to you particularly Chapter 1, which focuses on understanding that you are called to be a Levite. From Chapter 1 to Chapter 7, we find that we too are called to go behind the veil, to tear down strongholds, to lift our hands in praise and worship and to lift up our hearts unto the Lord; indeed, as He transforms us and makes us His holy people, the bride of Christ, the light of the world.

Some 2000 years ago, 120 disciples were in an upper room and received fire. In 1906, fire fell again in North America. The world is waiting on tiptoe for the fire to continue to fall. Thank you, Bishop Searight, for your contribution to the power and the magnanimity of praise and worship. Your sincere heart is refreshing to us all.

Your father in faith, I am so godly proud of this work.

Bishop Donald Hilliard, II
Senior Pastor – Cathedral International Church

INTRODUCTION

HAVE YOU EVER STOPPED by someone's house who was not expecting you? Although something told you to call first, you decided that your relationship was beyond a mere phone call. When you arrive, you eagerly walk to the door and ring the bell. No one answers. You peak inside the window and think, "Didn't I just hear the television?" You decide to ring the bell again, but this time you are pressing the bell a little longer. "Maybe he is in the shower," you try to reason. However, again, there is no answer. By now, you have become curious and frustrated. You peek into the garage and see the car. You decide to try one more time, but you knock this time. Still, there is no answer and you walk away feeling empty. You wonder what happened to the relationship.

Afterwards, you cannot believe that he would do this to you. You have *only* known him for ten years. As you drive away, you begin to think, "What is wrong with him? Didn't he hear me knocking on the door?" Finally, it dawns on you. A year ago, you started hanging with people from the job. You no longer had time for anyone else. You can hardly believe that a whole year has passed and you miss the relationship you once had.

Although this is a dramatization, it is similar to what you may experience in your relationship with God. You can become preoccupied with your life and forget the purpose for which God created you—to dwell with Him. Your prayer life decreases slowly and finally comes to a complete halt. You no longer read the Word. It is merely something you grab on your way out the door on Sunday mornings. It is not that you have stopped going to church...You have stopped becoming the church.

FIRST THINGS FIRST

Many times, you become preoccupied with everything else in your life: family, school, work, friends, vacations, material possessions, and other areas of focus. You rarely find time to communicate with God, until you have reached the lowest point in your life. Then you follow the same scenario discussed earlier. You go to church, this time expecting to experience the presence of God because *you are desperate* to commune with Him. When you do not feel the glory, you think, "The worship leader is not hitting it today." You close your eyes again and try to focus, but something is missing. You think, "Maybe next Sunday I'll have an experience with God." However, during the week, you do not set aside time to seek His face and Sunday rolls around again. Once more, you try to enter into His presence; however, you do not feel that same connection. This time you think, "If they would only sing my song, then I would be able to enter into His presence." Again, you walk away from the service feeling empty. You try to rationalize and decide that it is the pastor's fault that you have lost interest. You begin to blame everything on everyone...except yourself.

The truth of the matter is, if the corporate body is going to experience the glory of God, it must first be experienced individually. As a worship leader, it is essential to experience the glory of God in your personal life. If the body of Christ is going to be a light to the world, we must understand that the call to ministry is not just for the pastors, ministers and elders. The call is placed upon all of us—the worship team, the choir members, the musicians, the dancers, the ushers, the media team, the greeters and the security team. Each of these distinct roles is what I describe as the Sanctuary Ministries, because they all play an important part in the worship experience. Therefore, each member of the Sanctuary Ministries is a worship leader in his or her perspective role. Furthermore, it only takes one member to be out of place to affect the worship experience. You have a responsibility to seek after God with such a contagious enthusiasm for His presence, whereby your fire for God will catch hold in the earth.

Yes, you will experience the glory of God in every area of your life. More importantly, whomever you meet will see the glory that is upon your life. This glory will allow you to be a light in the world. When you truly understand this call to ministry, then you will see the real manifestation of God's presence. I am not saying that you are not experiencing the glory of the Lord now in the corporate experience. If you spent more time becoming the church on a personal level, you would develop a relationship with Him that transcends *your* life and *your* needs. You will become *The Dwelling Place* for God's presence. You will then find that your worship experience will go beyond the natural, ordinary day-to-day concerns. You will experience God in such a way that it will affect those around you. You will see blind eyes open, the deaf hear, and the lame walk. This will happen because you have had an experience with Him. It will be through your life that the glory of the Lord will stretch forth throughout the land and He will be magnified in great power and strength!

HEAR THE CALL TO WORSHIP

God is calling you into His glory as He did Moses in Exodus 24:15-16. It says,

> *"Then Moses climbed up the mountain, and the cloud covered it. And the glory of the Lord settled down on Mount Sinai, and the cloud covered it for six days. On the seventh day the Lord called to Moses from inside the cloud."*[1]

In order for God to minister to Moses, He had to call him away from the people and up into the mountain. While Moses was on the mountain, he fervently sought God for six days. Make no mistake about it. Moses went up into the mountain because he had a relationship with the Father. His ears were in tune to God's voice so that he could hear the call. Can you imagine the level of sensitivity that Moses had to the voice and the move of God? As a worship leader, you must become so in tune to God that you are able to hear His call. This sensitivity will only come out of your relationship with Him. You are going to have to be like Moses and move away from the noise. You must move away from your own desires of wanting to fit in. You are going to have to move away from the every day hustle of life and place your focus on Him.

DRAWING CLOSER TO GOD IS A CHOICE

The truth of the matter is that Moses had a choice. Yes, God called him. However, Moses could have chosen to hang out with everyone else. He could have acted as if he did not hear God, because he was more concerned with people. He could have been more concerned with the insecurity of having a speech impediment. He could have felt unworthy. Despite the people or his feelings, Moses chose to heed the voice of God and obey.

John 10:1-5 says,

"Let me set this before you as plainly as I can. If a person climbs over or through the fence of a sheep pen instead of going through the gate, you know he's up to no good—a sheep rustler! The shepherd walks right up to the gate. The gatekeeper opens the gate to him and the sheep recognize his voice. He calls his own sheep by name and leads them out. When he gets them all out, he leads them and they follow because they are familiar with his voice. They won't follow a stranger's voice but will scatter because they aren't used to the sound of it."[2]

I want to warn you not to sway from your mission when you hear the stranger's voice. You may be thinking, "Who is the stranger?" The stranger can be your flesh or it can be your lustful desires. The stranger can be your desire to be like the world. Ultimately, the stranger can be anything that pulls you away or drowns out the sound of God's voice in your life. It is up to you to hear His voice and to be led by it. Therefore, it is God's desire that you know His voice. You have to make the decision to hear His voice and obey. As in the scripture, God is calling you to the mountain experience and you must make the decision to adhere to His call.

If you look back at Exodus 24:15-16, you will see that the cloud also covered Moses as a form of protection. He was not able to see what was going on with the Israelites. He was not preoccupied with Joshua. He did not have to worry about his enemies coming after him, because God sent the cloud to surround him. The Bible says in Exodus 24:16 that the glory of the Lord settled down or rested on Mt. Sinai. With everything that is going on in your life, are you ready for God to send a cloud to rest on you? His glory will cover you from distractions. It will cover you from the darts of the enemy. You will be protected against the wear and tear of every day life. His glory will cover you while you move towards His perfect will. God is calling you to this same mountain experience, because He wants to develop a divine connection with you that will transform you into His image.

TRUE WORSHIP COMES OUT OF YOUR DESIRE FOR HIM

I am sure that it is not a surprise when I say that God wants you to become more like Him. John 4:23-24 says,

> *"It's who you are and the way you live that count before God. Your worship must engage your spirit in the pursuit of truth. That's the kind of people the Father is out looking for: those who are simply and honestly themselves before him in their worship. God is sheer being itself—Spirit. Those who worship him must do it out of their very being, their spirits, their true selves, in adoration."*[3]

You must worship God out of your very being. This means that your very being must be like Him. Therefore, you must have a desire and a strong will to be like Him. Philippians 2:13 says, *"For God is working in you, giving you the desire and the power to do what pleases him."*[4] This means that God has already given you the desire; you must be willing to live out that desire. He has already equipped you with the power; you must be willing to use it. If you are going to please God in your worship, your worship must be expressed through your desire for the truth. Many times, you may try to worship God out of your feelings or your flesh. However, God is calling you to the mountain, because He wants you to develop spiritually.

YOUR SPIRIT SEEKS AFTER THE TRUTH

Philippians 2:13 says that your worship must engage your spirit in the pursuit of truth. This means that your spirit seeks the truth. Remember, God has already placed the desire within you; it is your mind that has to change. Your mind has to want the truth. Your mind has to make the decision to follow the truth so that you can seek Him honestly. If you are going to be an effective worship leader, you must first be honest with yourself so that you can go before God without wrath or shame. It is through your sincere desire to be like God, that you will be able to worship Him and effectively participate in the worship experience.

While Moses waited in the cloud, the Lord called Moses out of the midst of the cloud. Exodus 24:17 says,

> *"The sight of the glory of the Lord was like a consuming fire on the top of the mountain in the eyes of the children of Israel."*[5]

What a glorious day when you experience the call from the midst of the cloud and into the glory of the Lord. Beloved, God wants to take you far beyond your mere imagination and into the place that He has prepared. It is in that place where He wants your life to glow with His consuming fire.

YOU NEED THE TOOLS TO BECOME AN EFFECTIVE WORSHIP LEADER

It is not a mystery that God desires to dwell within you. However, you must do your part. You must build a sanctuary or *The Dwelling Place* for Him in your life so that His glory can be revealed to the corporate body. How do you build *The Dwelling Place*? You construct

The Dwelling Place by obtaining the tools that will make you an effective worship leader. It will be through your sincerity that you will be able to create the atmosphere that is worthy of His presence. In order to develop this atmosphere, you must understand how the pattern, the people and the presence of God work together to create the environment for God to dwell amongst His people.

It is my hope that you will truly understand that God desires for you to experience the fullness of His glory. He doesn't want you to walk away from the worship experience empty, as in the story mentioned at the beginning of this introduction. He wants to develop a relationship with you that transcends beyond the superficial and into the spiritual.

You may be wondering, "How do you move into this place of experiencing His glory?" It is through Christ that you will experience the glory of the Lord in every area of your life. Ephesians 1:11-12 says,

> *"It's in Christ that we find out who we are and what we are living for. Long before we first heard of Christ and got our hopes up, he had his eye on us, had designs on us for glorious living, part of the overall purpose he is working out in everything and everyone."*[6]

In order for you to experience the glorious living as described in the scripture, you will have to know Christ in His sufferings. You will have to become cognizant of his glorious, morally sound attributes and infinite perfection. You will have to learn of His character. Once you know Him, you will desire to be like Him. Your transformation into His likeness will be the evidence of your relationship with God. It will be through this relationship that His glory will be revealed in every area of your life and in the world.

I pray that this book will challenge you to live a life that is pleasing to the Lord. This lifestyle will set you apart for the work of the Lord. It will enable you to build *The Dwelling Place* for His presence in your life. As a result, you will see the glory of the Lord spill out of your personal life and will spread like a consuming fire throughout the world.

ENDNOTES

1. New Living Translation.
2. The Message Bible.
3. The Message Bible.
4. New Living Translation.
5. New King James Version.
6. The Message Bible.

Chapter One

You Are Called to Be a Levite

CAN YOU IMAGINE GOING to your favorite restaurant and the host is nowhere to be found? After finding your own seat, you realize that there are only two waiters. Once the waiter finally takes your order, you learn that the cook has stepped out for a few minutes and the wait is going to be longer than usual. Although this is an exaggeration, it shows the importance of everyone being in place and functioning in his or her role.

YOU MUST UNDERSTAND YOUR ROLE AS A LEVITE

I am sure that you have heard that worshippers are called to be Levites. In this chapter, I will discuss the role and responsibilities of the Levites as it relates to worship and the Sanctuary Ministries. [As a side note, I want to reiterate that when I use the term "worship leader" throughout this book, I am referring to each member of the Sanctuary Ministries: worship team, choir members, musicians, dancers, greeters, ushers, media team, and security.]

The Levites were descendants of the tribe of Levi, one of the twelve sons of Israel. Levi had three sons: Gershon, Kohath and Merari. The name Levi means *he shall accompany*.[1] Their principle roles in the Temple included singing Psalms during Temple services, performing construction and maintenance for the Temple, serving as guards, and performing other services. Levites served as teachers, judges, and maintaining cities of refuge.[2] The Levites also served as the honor guards, gatekeepers, and musicians of the Temple.[3]

THE LEVITES MUST WORK TOGETHER

It is time that the Sanctuary Ministries understand the call of the Levite and work together to create the ultimate worship experience. The faces of the greeters are the first seen when entering the church. Greeters must smile and make everyone feel welcome. The ushers must be skillful in assigning seats. It is important that there are little distractions on the rows closest to the pulpit. At times, I believe that the ushers have one of the most challenging positions, because of the very nature of the job. However, it is important that ushers maintain self-control amidst the challenges. The security team is important as well. The security team makes sure that no one becomes unruly or causes harm to God's people. The worship team must lead the people through song and the expressions of worship. The musicians must be able to flow with the move of God and work in harmony with the worship team and the dancers. The dancers must be coordinated with all of the sanctuary ministries; they must work with the worship team and musicians. They must also coordinate their positioning with the ushers to maintain the flow of the service and work with the media team with any music needed. Finally, a skilled media team is responsible for the sound and recording the service.

AS A LEVITE YOU ARE CONSECRATED FOR THE WORK OF THE LORD

Now I am going to explain to you the importance of the role of the Levites. The Levites carried the sanctified vessels of the Tabernacle.

If the sanctified vessels were mishandled, the Levites' risked death. Therefore, the Levites had to be set apart for the work of the Lord. This is why it is important to present your body as a living sacrifice, holy and acceptable unto God. Romans 12:1 says that your reasonable service is to live holy and acceptable unto God. In the Message Bible, it says:

> *"So here's what I want you to do, God helping you: Take your everyday, ordinary life—your sleeping, eating, going-to-work, and walking-around life—and place it before God as an offering. Embracing what God does for you is the best thing you can do for him. Don't become so well-adjusted to your culture that you fit into it without even thinking. Instead, fix your attention on God. You'll be changed from the inside out. Readily recognize what he wants from you, and quickly respond to it. Unlike the culture around you, always dragging you down to its level of immaturity, God brings the best out of you, develops well-formed maturity in you".*[4]

God is calling you to be a well-formed, mature Christian. You cannot worship with the spirits of lust, fornication, pornography, envy, hatred, and malice in your heart. If you were back in the Old Testament, you would die trying to handle the sanctified vessels with sin in your heart, but thanks be unto God whose mercies are new every morning. Robert Davidson wrote a song that says, *"The steadfast love of the Lord never ceases. His mercies never come to an end, for they are new every morning. New every morning. Great is thy faithfulness, Oh Lord. Great is thy faithfulness".*[5]

YOU ARE REQUIRED TO BE FAITHFUL

Since God is faithful, it is important that you respond with faithfulness. I know that it is easy to rely on the mercies of God; however, you cannot allow the mercies of God to become a crutch for you to live a sinful lifestyle. You must decide that you will live a holy lifestyle. If the corporate body is going to experience a mighty move of His power, you must be the first partaker of the sanctity of God. You cannot lead the people of God as a dirty vessel.

Psalm 34 is the psalm of application. It challenges you to apply the Word of God to your life. It reads:

"I bless God every chance I get; my lungs expand with his praise.
I live and breathe GOD; if things aren't going well, hear this and be happy:
Join me in spreading the news; together let's get the word out.
GOD met me more than halfway; he freed me from my anxious fears.
Look at him; give him your warmest smile. Never hide your feelings from him.
When I was desperate, I called out, and GOD got me out of a tight spot.
GOD's angel sets up a circle of protection around us while we pray.
Open your mouth and taste, open your eyes and see—how good GOD is. Blessed are you who run to him.
Worship GOD if you want the best; worship opens doors to all his goodness.
Young lions on the prowl get hungry, but GOD-seekers are full of God.

Come, children, listen closely; I'll give you a lesson in God worship.
Who out there has a lust for life? Can't wait each day to come upon beauty?
Guard your tongue from profanity, and no more lying through your teeth.
Turn your back on sin; do something good. Embrace peace—don't let it get away!
GOD keeps an eye on his friends, his ears pick up every moan and groan.
GOD won't put up with rebels; he'll cut them from the pack.
Is anyone crying for help? GOD is listening, ready to rescue you.
If your heart is broken, you'll find GOD right there; if you're kicked in the gut, he'll help you catch your breath.
Disciples so often get into trouble; still, GOD is there every time.
He's your bodyguard, shielding every bone; not even a finger gets broken.
The wicked commit slow suicide; they waste their lives hating the good.
GOD pays for each slave's freedom; no one who runs to him loses out."[6]

In this scripture, you can see that God is calling you to live a life that is pleasing to Him. When you become a God seeker—you become full of God. You become full of His promises. You become full of faith. So when you worship God, you will receive the best from Him. You will receive all of the promises that He has set for you. However, you must do your part. God has provided you with everything that you need to live holy, now it is up to you. As a worshipper, if you are going to build *The Dwelling Place* during the corporate experience, your lifestyle must become His dwelling place.

TO BE AN EFFECTIVE WORSHIP LEADER YOU MUST BE SPIRITUALLY FIT

I would like to take a moment and look back at the Levites. The Levites had to be spiritually fit because they were *guardians of the tabernacle.*[7] Numbers 18:23-24 reads:

> *Henceforth the Israelites shall not come near the Tent of Meeting [covered sanctuary, the Holy Place, and the Holy of Holies], lest they incur guilt and die. But the Levites shall do the [menial] service of the Tent of Meeting, and they shall bear and remove the iniquity of the people [that is, be answerable for the legal pollutions of the holy things and offer the necessary atonements for unintentional offenses in these matters.]*[8]

In this scripture, you can see that the Israelites could not come near the Tent of Meeting. The Levites were the ones who assisted the priests and served in the temple. Today if you are going to build *The Dwelling Place*, you must be spiritually prepared to serve in the worship service. Although the role of the worship leader may seem high and lifted up, the actual call of the worship leader is to be a servant. In order to see the move of God, you must be in the position of humility. Worship is not centered around man-made agendas. It is, however, about positioning yourself and the corporate body to enter into His presence.

PREPARATION PLACES YOU IN POSITION FOR WORSHIP

You can position yourself through preparation. To position yourself and the corporate body is to prepare for the presence of God. You prepare for worship by living sanctified and holy. It is through your preparation that you are equipped to enter into His presence. This preparation will cause worship to become part of your lifestyle. You should not experience worship only on Sunday mornings or during mid-week services. You should be a worshipper 24 hours a day, 365 days a year—living in a continual state of worship.

A CONSCIOUSNESS OF GOD MOVES YOU INTO A CONTINUAL STATE OF WORSHIP

How can you move into this continual state of worship? I believe that this is accomplished by having a consciousness of God and a fundamental awareness of the move of God in your life. Furthermore, I believe that you can stay in this continual state of worship through the anointing of God. The anointing gives a fundamental awareness of God's presence and glory. A great deal of preparation for worship and functionality of the worshipper have a lot to do with the anointing. Once you have prepared for worship, the anointed oil is poured upon you in the corporate experience. I believe that once the anointed oil is poured on you, you will be loosed from the spirits of lust, hatred, and every sin mentioned earlier. The spirit of the Lord will dwell within you.

I would like to look at the Levites one last time. The Levites not only served in the Tabernacle, but they encamped around the tabernacle. Numbers 1:53 says,

"But the Levites will camp around the Tabernacle of the Covenant to offer the people of Israel protection from the Lord's fierce anger. The Levites are responsible to stand guard around the Tabernacle."[9]

When the Tabernacle was erected at a new location, God commanded that the tribes settle around it in a specific order:

On the East side: Judah, Issachar and Zebulun
On the South side: Reuben, Simeon and Gad
On the West side: Ephraim and Manasseh
(the sons of Joseph) and Benjamin
On the North side: Dan, Asher, and Naphtali[10]

If the corporate body of believers is going to truly enter the glory of God, everyone must be in place. If no one is available to work the sound, then the people of God will not be able to hear. If the singers are not in place, then a part will be missing. If the ushers are not available to manage the flow of the people into the service, then that leaves room for havoc.

YOU ARE IMPORTANT TO THE WORSHIP EXPERIENCE

Each Sanctuary Ministry has its place in the service and contributes to its success. The worship experience is hindered when the sound or singers is missing. I believe that it does affect the level of the anointing. I am not saying that God will not show up. What I am saying is that as a Levite, you can intensify the worship experience for the corporate body or create a normal, business as usual experience. This business as usual worship experience does not give the opportunity for the unusual to happen. It gives way for the ordinary worship experience week after week. When everyone is in place, I believe that God's presence is maximized and the corporate body will experience an unusual phenomenon.

ENDNOTES

1. The Role of the Levites. The Tribe The Cohen-Levi Family Heritage Page. http://www.cohen-levi.org/the_levites/role_of_the_levites.htm.
2. Levite Page. Levite-Wikipedia, the free encyclopedia. http://en.wikipedia.org/wiki/Levite.
3. The Role of the Levites.
4. The Message Bible.
5. The Steadfast Love of the Lord by Robert Davidson. Tabs Lyrics and Cords page.http://www.tabslyricschords.com/mostlychristian/The%20Steadfast%20Love%20Of%20The%20Lord.TXT.
6. The Message Bible.
7. Levite page. Web Bible Encyclopedia-ChristianAnswers.net page. http://www.christiananswers.net/dictionary/levite.html.
8. Amplified Bible.
9. New Living Translation.
10. The Levites (Numbers 3:3-37). The Levites page. http://www.domini.org/tabern/levites.htm.

Chapter Two

The Call to Worship

IMAGINE THIS... YOU ARE on your way to see a Broadway Musical. You are so excited because you purchased your tickets over a year ago and today is the day. Once you get to your seat, you start looking at the program. You can hardly wait because the show received rave reviews. Suddenly, the lights go out and there is an announcement. Tonight they decided to do an experiment. Members of the orchestra will now play the roles of the actors. The actors will take on the administrative roles while the director and stage crew play the instruments.

Under normal circumstances, you are an adventurous person. However, tonight you are expecting to see the show that you have heard so much about. "Ok, maybe this is all a part of the act," you try to rationalize. However, when the show begins, you notice that the lights begin to flicker. You find out that the actors cannot agree on who should be the director. Sounding horrible is just one of the issues facing the orchestra. The newly made orchestra is half-empty because most of the stagehands did not come to work. The actors, now played by the musicians, have absolutely no clue of how to act. Needless to say, the night was a complete circus and you are ready for a refund.

WORSHIP REQUIRES ORDER, FAITHFULNESS & ABILITY

Although this is a dramatization, it is a great illustration to show that there is an order to worship. There is a level of faithfulness required for worship and an ability to express praise in worship. All three components are a vital part of the worship experience. In 1 Chronicles 25:1, 6, it says,

> *"Moreover David and the captains of the host separated to the service of the sons of Asaph, and of Heman, and of Jeduthun, who should prophesy with harps, with psalteries, and with cymbals: and the number of the workmen according to their service was:...All these were under the hands of their father for song in the house of the LORD, with cymbals, psalteries, and harps, for the service of the house of God, according to the king's order to Asaph, Jeduthun, and Heman."*[1]

In 1 Chronicles 25, David appointed the singers and musicians to prophesy in the temple. In verse 6, it says that *all these were under the order of their father*. The word "order" shows that David directed the worship service. This is a key point for you to understand. The corporate experience of worship must flow from the pastor. If the corporate body of believers is going to experience the mighty move of God, each believer must be willing to submit to the father of the house. You cannot override your pastor. You cannot go above your pastor. If you are going to build a dwelling place for God's presence, you must come under the authority of your pastor, who is the voice of God for the house.

YOU MUST COME UNDER AUTHORITY IN WORSHIP

I know that the word *authority* may be a tough pill to swallow. Society has a problem with authority and, unfortunately, this problem has trickled into the church. However, you must be different. You must be able to submit to the authority of your pastor. Instead of talking about him when he makes a mistake, learn to pray for him. As a leader, it is difficult to be right all the time. You must learn to love your pastor unconditionally. The truth of the matter is that you are not right all the time. So why put that expectation on someone else? Learn to be patient, understanding, and maintain self-control. When you are able to work in harmony with your pastor, you will position yourself for the miraculous.

If you look back at the scripture, it says that they came together under the authority of three tribes: Asaph, Heman, and Jeduthun. So when the call was made for worship, the people came under the authority of these three tribes.

THE TRIBE OF ASAPH

I would like to look at the first tribe, Asaph. The name Asaph means *to collect* or *to come together.* This does not mean that you can simply come together because it is the annual conference. You have to come under the authority of Asaph. In the scripture, they did not receive special privileges because of their status. It did not matter where they worked, because under the name Asaph they had no choice in the matter. What that means for you as a worship leader is that you have to eliminate the options. The Pastor should not have to ask, if you can come to service. I understand if you have to work or go to school. However, if you just do not feel like going to church, then that is childish and immature behavior. It is His will and word that you worship with the corporate body. When you read this particular text you must understand the authority of coming together. It doesn't matter what the problem is, you have to find a way to get to the house of God.

YOU ARE REQUIRED TO WORSHIP WITH THE COLLECTIVE BODY

I would like to take you to Acts 4:31 to show the importance of coming to the house of the Lord. It says,

> *"And when they had prayed, the place was shaken where they were assembled together; and they were all filled with the Holy Ghost, and they spake the word of God with boldness."*[2]

This scripture illustrates the power of coming together. Since they assembled together, they were all filled with the Holy Ghost. I am sure that God could have filled them privately. However, when God wants to show forth His greatness, he wants it witnessed by the multitude. What effect would His power have if just one person was filled with the Holy Ghost at home? The others would have looked at him as if he had lost his mind. When everyone came together, God moved and they were all filled. Each one had an experience with God. If you are going to experience the mighty move of God's glory, you must go to church. This is not to say that you cannot worship God in your home, because worship must be incorporated in every area of your life. If you stay home, you will miss the anointed oil that is poured on the corporate body.

When you begin to understand the importance of coming together, you will also understand that your presence is vital to the kingdom of

God. In Ephesians 4:16, it says,

> *"From whom the whole body fitly joined together and compacted by that which every joint supplieth, according to the effectual working in the measure of every part, maketh increase of the body unto the edifying of itself in love."*[3]

In the scripture, it says that every joint supplies. In your body, your joint allows you to *stretch, swivel, pivot, and point. Your body can perform more than one kind of motion because of the joints.*[4] I want you to understand that you are a joint in the body of Christ. When you are not at church, the body cannot function at its full capacity. Can you imagine what would happen if the joint between your hand and forearm decided not to work? You would lose mobility in your hand. Maybe you would call it arthritis and thus movement of your hand would be limited, stiff, and painful. This is just like with the body of Christ. If you are not in your place, the body loses its ability to stretch and point. There may be a moment when a member of the body needs your love. However, you are nowhere to be found and, subsequently, the body loses its ability to be flexible to the move of God in that area. If you are a part of the body of Christ, you must function in that manner.

YOUR PRESENCE IS NECESSARY

If you wonder why it seems that the corporate experience is limited, it is because it is functioning at a low mobility rate. How can you touch the life of your sister or brother when you are not at home? I know that you can call on the phone or send an email. However, there is nothing like your presence being made perfect in the glory of God. Through the glory of God, you can show forth love, healing, and strength to your sister or brother in Christ. If you are going to truly build a dwelling place for the presence of God, then you must come under the authority of Asaph. Always remember that you are a vital part to the body of Christ.

THE TRIBE OF HEMAN

Now I would like to look at the second tribe, Heman. The name Heman means *faithful*. This means that they were full of faith. In order for you to be faithful in your role as a worship leader, you must be full of faith. It does not matter what's going on in your life, you have something that drives you into the direction of where God wants you to be. He is calling for you to be faithful, not because you are asked to be at service. He is calling you to be faithful, because you understand the call that is upon your life. You will show up for service when you are not asked because of the call that is placed upon your life. It is through your act of faithfulness, that your faith is ignited. It is through your connection with God that you can believe in the miraculous phenomenon of God's glory.

Hebrews 11:1-3 gives the definition of faith. It says,

"Now faith is the assurance (the confirmation, the title deed) of things [we] hope for, being the proof of things [we] do not see and the conviction of their reality [faith perceiving as real fact what is not revealed to the senses]. For by [faith—trust and holy fervor born of faith] the men of old had divine testimony borne to them and obtained a good report. By faith we understand that the worlds [during the successive ages] were framed (fashioned, put in order, and equipped for their intended purpose) by the word of God, so that what we see was not made out of things which are visible."[5]

Here in the scripture you can see that faith is described as the title deed. In real estate, a deed is a document that is sealed as an instrument of bond, contract, or conveyance especially relating to property.[6] When you look back at the scripture it says that your faith becomes the instrument that binds your belief system with reality. It is through your act of faith that God conveys his promises.

YOU MUST HAVE FAITH & BELIEVE

It is important that your faith be kindled through the development of your relationship with God. How can you minister healing, when you do not believe that He is a healer? People are coming to the church broken and bruised, needing a touch from God. You must be in the position to believe that God can move mountains. It is more than just a song. It is more than just notes on a keyboard. It is more than just movements in dance. It is more than just seating the congregation. Furthermore, it is more than just equalizing the sound. You are creating the atmosphere for the supernatural. Therefore, if the church is going to experience the matchless power of God, we must believe. Allow your faith to become the instrument that binds someone's miracle.

If you look further in the scripture to verse 4, it says,

"[Prompted, actuated] by faith Abel brought God a better and more acceptable sacrifice than Cain, because of which it was testified of him that he was righteous [that he was upright and in right standing with God], and God bore witness by accepting and acknowledging his gifts. And though he died, yet [through the incident] he is still speaking. [Gen 4:3-10]"[7]

You can see that Abel was made righteous by his faith. As a worshipper, your faith will cause you to be in right standing with God. Your faith will take you where your talent cannot go. Your faith will move you from being just an ordinary worship leader, to being a righteous worship leader.

YOUR FAITH WILL MAKE YOU RIGHTEOUS BEFORE GOD

If you look back at the scripture, you will not only see that Abel was made righteous, but God also accepted his gifts. Are you wondering why the glory of the Lord is not falling like in the days of old? Are you righteous in the sight of God? Does your worship reach the very throne room of God? Are you actively engaged in worship through your faith or are you an observer taking up space? Beloved, it is time that you move from the ordinary worship experience into the extraordinary. God wants to take you beyond your current position. If you look back at the scripture, you will see that it was because of Abel's faith that his voice still cried out from the ground after his death. If you look back at Gen 4:10, it said that Abel's blood cried out from the ground. Can you imagine having such faith that it [your faith] lives on after [your] death? Glory to God! Can you imagine what will happen when your prayers for your grandchildren are heard by God after you are long gone? Because of your righteousness, can you imagine your prayers calling out to God, exactly when your children's children needed it the most? Your faith supersedes your imagination and goes where you cannot see.

This is why in Hebrews 11:6, it says:

"But without faith it is impossible to please and be satisfactory to Him.

For whoever would come near to God must [necessarily] believe that God exists and that He is the rewarder of those who earnestly and diligently seek Him [out]." [8]

If you want to be able to build The Dwelling Place for God, you must be able to draw near unto Him. As a worshipper, it is important that you are pleasing unto God. If He is going to accept your worship, you must live a life of faith. It does not say, without talent, you cannot please Him. It says without faith, you cannot please Him. This means that you cannot live an unrighteous lifestyle and expect God to accept your worship. Your talent means nothing to God. He gave it to you anyway. Although you use your talent for His glory, you cannot make His name glorious in the earth if you are not pleasing to Him. Everything that you are doing will be in vain. All of your singing, playing, dancing and serving in ministry will be done for your own glory.

YOUR FAITH WILL HELP TO CREATE THE ATMOSPHERE FOR WORSHIP

I want to challenge you in the area of your faith. This is vital to your role as a worship leader. It is through your faith that you create the atmosphere for the glory of the Lord to dwell. It is by your faith that the lame will walk. It is by your faith that a wayward child will return home. It is by your faith that broken marriages will be put back together. I pray that the faith of God will be spawned in your heart, mind, and spirit.

THE TRIBE OF JEDUTHUN

The last tribe that I want to draw your attention to is the tribe of Jeduthun. The name Jeduthun means *to express praise*. If you want to experience His glory, and I am not talking about knowing how to have church; I mean true glory... You will have to come under the authority of Jeduthun. This means that while you are on your way to church you are expressing praise. It is not something that you do mechanically; however, the praise is within you.

Psalms 100 says,

"Make a joyful noise unto the Lord, all ye lands! Serve the Lord with gladness! Come before His presence with singing! Know (perceive, recognize, and understand with approval) that the Lord is God! It is He who has made us, not we ourselves [and we are His]! We are His people and the sheep of His pasture. Enter into His gates with thanksgiving and a thanks offering and into His courts with praise! Be thankful and sing to Him, bless and affectionately praise His name! For the Lord is good; His mercy and loving-kindness are everlasting, His faithfulness and truth endure to all generations."[9]

In the scripture, you see that praise is expressed out of your knowledge of who He is. When the praises of God go forth, you cannot just stand and watch. You must actively participate. As a singer, you must express praise through your words. As a musician, you express praise through the notes. As a dancer, you express praise through movements. As a member of the media team, you express praise through your skill. As a greeter, usher and security team member, you express praise through your attitude. All of these Sanctuary Ministries express praise through the act of serving in the Lords church and by being an active participant in the worship experience. This is why the scripture says let everything praise Him.

YOU MUST COME UNDER THE AUTHORITY OF ASAPH, HEMAN AND JEDUTHUN

As a worship leader, you must come under the authority of all three: Asaph, Heman and Jeduthun. If you look back at 1 Chronicles 25, you will see that when the tribes came together, they were as one. They were not fighting amongst themselves. They all came together to create one sound unto God. It is through your submission to the authority and move of God that you will be able to build a dwelling place for His presence.

ENDNOTES

1. King James Version
2. King James Version.
3. King James Version.
4. Joints. The Human Body Page. http://library.thinkquest.org/5777/ske7.htm
5. Amplified Bible.
6. Deed. Dictionary.com. http://dictionary.reference.com/browsee/deed.
7. Amplified Bible.
8. Amplified Bible.
9. Amplified Bible.

Chapter Three

GOD IS LOOKING FOR YOU

HAVE YOU EVER GONE to buy a new puppy from a breeder? Although the puppies may look similar, only one will capture your heart. This is what happened with one of the greatest worshippers in the Bible. In Psalm 89:20 God said, "I have found my David." Can you imagine God searching the entire earth looking for him? There were many for God to choose from. Even David's father, Jesse, did not think that he was the one Samuel was looking for. However, God's hand was upon David. It is amazing to think that God did not look among the princes to find David, but he looked among the people…the ordinary people and found a shepherd.

WHY GOD WAS LOOKING FOR DAVID

Why was God looking for David? I believe that God was looking for David because there was a place missing in the heart of God. Before Satan was kicked out of heaven, he was the minstrel in the presence of God. Ezekiel 28:12-15 says:

"You had everything going for you.
You were in Eden, God's garden.
You were dressed in splendor,
your robe studded with jewels:

Carnelian, peridot, and moonstone,
beryl, onyx, and jasper,
Sapphire, turquoise, and emerald,
all in settings of engraved gold.
A robe was prepared for you
the same day you were created.
You were the anointed cherub.
I placed you on the mountain of God.
You strolled in magnificence
among the stones of fire.
From the day of your creation
you were sheer perfection..."[1]

From the day of Lucifer's creation, he captured the heart of God. He was the anointed cherub. As a cherub, Lucifer was not only a symbol of God's Holy presence, but he was also anointed and guarded the very presence of God. As a musician, he ministered before the very throne of God. After Lucifer was thrown out of heaven, there was something missing in God's heart. God longed for the sound, the beauty, and the perfection that can only be found in His presence...until He found David.

CAN YOU CAPTURE THE HEART OF GOD?

So what was it about David that captured God's heart? In the scriptures, you will see that Christ came from the line or the seed of David. Again, I have to ask—what was it about David that God would allow such a great honor to befall him? What was it about David that God's only begotten Son would come from his seed? The answer—David was a mighty man of valor and courage, even in his early years as a shepherd. He was fearless and believed that with the help of God he could conquer any foe, even if it was a lion, a bear, or a giant. Amidst overwhelming adversity, he knew that God would take care of him and give great victory.

YOU ARE ANOINTED TO WORSHIP

There is no question that David was anointed. The Bible shares that David was anointed three times in his life. Firstly, he was anointed in 1 Samuel 16:1-13 by the priest/prophet Samuel at Jesse's house in Bethlehem. Secondly, he was anointed at Hebron after the death of King Saul, ruler of Judah in 2 Samuel 2:4. Lastly, in 2 Samuel 5:3, he was anointed king over Israel seven years later. God not only chose David, but anointed him for the position. This, for me, is a clear indication that we cannot do anything without the anointing of God. The ushers cannot direct the people of God. The greeters cannot welcome the people. The media team cannot regulate the sound. The security cannot guard the temple. The choir cannot sing. The musicians cannot play; neither can the dancers go forth without the anointing of God. The holy oil of God prepares each worshipper. It sanctifies and makes us holy for the assignments ahead. The holy oil of God's glory needs to permeate our very beings to take us from the ordinary to experiencing the extraordinary presence of God.

In my opinion, since God was looking for David, He was trying to fill the emptiness in His heart. When Lucifer was kicked out of heaven, it left a void. There was a void of music and worship. God created Lucifer with a divine purpose. However, Lucifer thought that the attention and the accolades that came with the position made him equal to God. He quickly learned that there was no other beside God and he was kicked out of the very presence of his Father and Creator. Although, God is sovereign He is also love and He longed for the anointed sound.

Just like David—There is a place in God's heart that only you can fill. Believe it, or not, you didn't just decide to be a worship leader. Before the very foundations of the earth, God had a divine purpose for your life. No one can take your place. No one can worship like you. No one can love God the way that you can. You must allow yourself to become vulnerable to the Holy Spirit so that God can search the very recesses of your soul. This connection will give you such a relationship with Him that it will be expressed in every area of your life.

WORSHIP ALLOWS YOU TO SEE FROM GOD'S PERSPECTIVE

I believe that because David was a worshipper, he received greater confidence than those around him. He began to see from God's perspective. Worship takes you out of your ordinary life and lifts you up to where He is. This is one of the reasons David was so successful. He understood that he was nothing in his own strength. It was through God, that he was able to conquer any mountain.

YOU CAN DEVELOP INTO AN EFFECTIVE WORSHIPPER

I would like to discuss three characteristics of David. I believe that these characteristics are important to you as a worshipper and should be incorporated into your life. They are as follows: 1) David was a shepherd, 2) David was a minstrel, and 3) David was a leader.

DAVID THE SHEPHERD

As mentioned earlier, David was anointed while he was a shepherd looking over his father's flock. The key here is that David had the responsibility of caring for something that did not belong to him. Technically, David did not own the sheep. Although he may have benefited from the sheep as Jesse's son, they still did not belong to him. Therefore, David's care and protection of his father's sheep clearly demonstrated his acceptance of the role.

ARE YOU READY TO LOVE BEYOND YOUR UNDERSTANDING?

As a worshipper, you must be willing to care for others. How can you truly love God when you cannot love your brother or sister that you see everyday? How can you worship God, when you look down on those who do not meet your standards? How can you truly worship God with malice and hatred in your heart? The answer—there is no way you can do it. You must be willing to love, even if it means that you are putting your feelings and emotions on the line. Even in my own experiences, I can remember choosing to love and even help those who mistreated me. It wasn't because I saw myself as being better or bigger. I chose and still choose to love because I realize that if I am truly going to be like God, I must love like Him. This by no means is easy, but when you challenge yourself in the area of love, you will be changed by love.

In Genesis 4:8-10 it says:

"Cain had words for his brother. They were out in the field; Cane came at Abel his brother and killed him.
God said to Cain; "Where is Abel your brother?" He said, "How should I know? Am I his babysitter?"[2]

Cain didn't understand that he had a responsibility to care for his brother. Instead, in his anger, he chose to murder him. Are you your brother's keeper? Absolutely, yes!!! In Genesis 8:10-12 it says:

> *"God said, "What have you done! The voice of your brother's blood is calling to me from the ground. From now on you'll get nothing but curses from this ground. You'll be driven from this ground; you'll be driven from this ground that has opened up its arms to receive the blood of your murdered brother. You'll farm this ground, but it will no longer give you its best. You'll be a homeless wanderer on earth."*[3]

In the scripture, it shows that you curse yourself when you choose to kill someone with words or with actions. Notice that murder is not just the act of killing someone. You can kill someone's spirit with your words. You can murder someone with your actions. You may be doing your best to grow spiritually and wondering, why there isn't tremendous growth taking place in you, as it is in others. You may even be successful in the corporate world, but you still feel emptiness in your heart. I would like to suggest that you check yourself. Check your heart and your motives. Are you a loving person? Are you open to love or are you closed and protective of your feelings? Do you care about the feelings and needs of others or does your life revolve around your feelings and your needs?

As worship leaders, you must understand that you have a responsibility to care for the people of God. Yes, God has given you the honor to serve His people with your gifts and talents. God has also given you a greater responsibility to love. You must become like a shepherd and lovingly touch the people of God through your life, your words, and your actions. As a worship leader, you must be touchable and approachable. You may think that this call is only for the pastor, elders, and ministers. However, I beg to differ. As a worship leader, you are called to take the people of God into the throne room of His presence. How can the people go, if they cannot connect with you? You must be willing to move beyond your insecurities and personal issues. If you are going to build *The Dwelling Place* for His presence, then you are going to have to become your brother's keeper by showing love to those whom God has placed in your care. This love must reach beyond the walls of the church and must be felt by everyone you touch.

DAVID THE MINSTREL

Soon after David was anointed by Samuel, he was sent to soothe Saul, who was being tormented by an evil spirit. 1 Samuel 16:23 says:

> *"And it came to pass, when the evil spirit from God was upon Saul, that David took a harp, and played with his hand; so Saul was refreshed and the evil spirit departed from him."*[4]

Early on, you saw that David was a worshipper and a minstrel. He worshipped until the evil spirit left Saul. This is so powerful. In the scripture, you can see the power that is manifested through David's ability to be an effective minstrel. Through his worship, Saul was refreshed and the evil spirit departed.

ARE YOU READY FOR HIS ANOINTING?

As a minstrel, you must be able to invoke the very presence of God until the captives are set free. This does not mean that you are the best singer or musician. Truthfully, there are singers who are ushers and members of other ministries. What is important, however, is that a minstrel is able to get God's attention. You must be able to minister until depression leaves. You must be able to minister until the yoke destroying power of God's presence changes lives. This is why it is so important for you to read the word of God, have a prayer life, and renew your mind. You must be spiritually fit to worship God and to be sensitive to His move. You must be able to choose the right song. You cannot sing a song about joy when the worship moment calls for brokenness and is bringing forth deliverance. Furthermore, you must be flexible enough to change with the Holy Spirit. The responsibility of the minstrel is more than just singing, playing, or dancing. It is about building a place for the presence of God to change, rearrange, and restore. It doesn't matter if you are on the third row of the choir or in the Media Room. You must be able to minister until the power of God falls and brings healing, salvation, deliverance, and life.

DAVID THE LEADER

Everyone loves a strong a leader. Everyone likes it when things are going great. You look around and success is everywhere. It seems like everything that the leader touches turns to gold. However, what happens when you do all you can and tragedy happens anyway? In 1 Samuel 30:1-6, David, the courageous leader, experiences a valley experience. It reads:

> *"Now it happened, when David and his men came to Ziklag, on the third day, that the Amalekites had invaded the South and Ziklag, attacked Ziklag and burned it with fire, and had taken captive the women and those who were there, from small to great; they did not kill anyone, but carried them away and went their way. So David and the people who were with him lifted up their voices and wept, until they had no more power to weep. And David's two wives, Ahinoam the Jezreelitess, and Abigail the widow of Nabal the Carmelite, had been taken captive. Now David was greatly distressed, for the people spoke of stoning him, because the soul of all the people was grieved,*

every man for his sons and his daughters."[5]

In the scripture, David and his men went to visit with the Philistines and returned to Ziklag. They found that their enemy, the Amalekites, had invaded Ziklag and burned the city to the ground. Moreover, they had taken all of the women and those who remained. The men became angry and wanted to stone David. I am sure they started playing the blame game. If they had not followed David, then they would have been able to protect their families. As a leader, this was one of the lowest points in David's life. However, verse 6 says that David encouraged himself in the Lord. He gathered 600 men and fought for their families.

CAN YOU LEAD EFFECTIVELY WHEN FACED WITH ADVERSITY?

As a worship leader, you are going to have to be prepared to fight in the spirit. There are going to be days when you are going to have your own struggles, disappointments, and fears. However, you are going to have to encourage yourself in the Lord and fight. "Fight for what?" you may ask. As a worship leader, you must realize that people are coming to church in search of answers. Despite your personal situations, are you able to lead the people of God into the presence of God? The truth is that when you look at the title of "worship leader", the second word is *leader*. Are you prepared to lead? People are looking for healing, deliverance, and strength. As a leader, you must understand that every time you minister in worship, you are waging war in the spirit for the lives of those God has entrusted in your hands. This is not just about you and your song list. If you are an usher, it is not about control. It is about being spiritually fit to fight the good fight of faith. You must be courageous and have the faith to believe that God can do the miraculous!

It is my desire that you really understand your call as a worship leader. God is indeed looking for you, just like the example of the puppies at the beginning of this chapter, where they all had similarities. You may have talents and gifts similar to someone else's. You may be better or you may be worse. Despite the level of your ability, you have a place in the heart of God. There is a place that only you can fill. Do not become discouraged because you feel overlooked. If your gift is placed in the forefront or if it's on the back row, God has not forgotten about you. You are vital to the kingdom of God.

Remember just like David, the hand of God is upon your life. It is vital that you develop spiritually, while perfecting your gift. I would like to encourage you to love like a shepherd, worship like a minstrel, and lead courageously. It is God's desire that you become a representation of His Holy presence in the earth.

ENDNOTES

1. The Message Bible.
2. The Message Bible.
3. The Message Bible.
4. King James Version.
5. New International Version – UK.

Chapter Four

CAN YOU RECOGNIZE HIM?

DO YOU REMEMBER WATCHING television as a popular artist begin to sing at a live concert? Once the artist appears, the crowd goes wild. Some began to jump, while others almost instinctively throw their hands in the air and cheer, because the artist has arrived. How can thousands of people from different cultures, social classes, and backgrounds come together and have the same response? That's simple. The common denominator is the artist and his music. Through the music, each fan feels that he knows the artist and can find himself in the lyrics.

YOUR KNOWLEDGE OF HIM WILL CAUSE YOU TO WORSHIP HIM

This, in itself, is an example of worship. Worship is derived out of your knowledge or ability to recognize something. John Calvin, a Protestant Reformist, described worship as,

> *"To know God is to be changed by God;*
> *True knowledge of God leads to worship."*[1]

When you think about it, how can you worship something or someone that you do not know? Even further, how can you know God without any evidence of change? It is impossible!

There must be signs in your life that attest to your change. The day is over where you can say, "Well, I'm like this because I'm just like my mother." In 2 Corinthians 5:16-17 it says,

> *"So from now on we regard no one from the worldly point of view. Though we once regarded Christ in this way, we do so no longer. Therefore, if anyone is in Christ, the new creation has come: The old has gone, the new is here!"*[2]

When you accepted the Lord Jesus Christ as your personal savior, you no longer had your old life. Although your physical appearance did not change, you were transformed in your spirit. God gave you another chance at life. He gave you the opportunity to live a more fulfilling life in His will. Just like you had to make the choice for salvation, it is up to you to change. It is time to exchange some negative behaviors, for godly behaviors. It is time that you move away from being an immature Christian and develop into a mature Christian.

This is vitally important to you as a worship leader. If you are going to lead the corporate body into the throne room of God, your life must testify that you know God. You cannot lead from where you have not gone. If you are going to be an effective worship leader, you must read the Word of God, remain in a constant state of prayer, and renew your mind.

YOU WILL RECOGNIZE HIM THROUGH HIS WORD

I am sure that you have heard many times that you must read your word. I am here to reiterate that fact. In Matthew 4:4, it says,

> *"But he answered and said, It is written, Man shall not live by bread alone, but by every word that proceedeth out of the mouth of God."*[3]

If you want to know God, you must know what He is saying. Right now, you may be looking to hear a word from the Lord regarding your life. I want to challenge you by asking, "What does His Word say?" The Word of God is more than just stories that happened over 2,000 years ago. In Psalms 119 it says that the Word of God is the lamp unto my feet and the light unto my pathway. How can you walk without the light of God guiding your way? I must share with you Psalm 119:105-112. It says,

> *"By your words I can see where I am going; they throw a beam of light on my dark path. I've committed myself and I'll never turn back from living by your righteous order. Everything's falling apart on me, God; put me together again with your Word. Festoon me with your finest sayings, God; teach me your holy rules. My life is as close as my own hands, but I don't forget what you have revealed. The wicked do their best to throw me off track, but I don't swerve an inch from my course. I inherited your book on living; its mine forever—what a gift! And how happy it makes me! I concentrate on doing exactly what you say—I always have and always will."*[4]

The Word of God is an inheritance. You may think of an inheritance as money, jewelry, or an estate. However, the Word of God is one of the greatest inheritances you can receive, because it has everything you need. In the scripture, it said, *"Put me together with your word."* Only the

Word of God can put you back together again when your life has been broken into pieces. Only the inheritance from your heavenly Father can mend your broken heart. The Word of God can uplift you when you are down. The Word of God gives you peace and guides your life. When you are in a spiritual warfare, you can use the Word of God as a weapon against the enemy. If you need healing, it is in the Word. Whatever the need, God has already provided the tools through His Word. If you want to be an effective worship leader, you must become a doer of the Word of God. As a leader, you will be able to use the Word in worship by declaring, *"Bless the Lord, O my soul! O Lord my God, You are very great: You are clothed with honor and majesty."*[5] There is great power in the Word of God that should be utilized more in the worship experience. I pray that you begin to understand the invaluable treasure that you have in the Word of God.

YOU WILL BE ABLE TO IDENTIFY HIM THROUGH PRAYER

Next, I would like to challenge you in the area of prayer. In 1 Thessalonians 5:16-18 says:

> *"Be cheerful no matter what; pray all the time; thank God no matter what happens. This is the way God wants you who belong to Christ Jesus to live."*[6]

Again, I am sure that you have heard that you should pray without ceasing. This means that you are supposed to live a life of continual prayer. Through prayer, you will develop a closer relationship with Him. This relationship will go beyond the superficial; praying only when you need Him. You will move into having an intimate relationship with God, wherein you can actually say that you know His voice.

In Luke 24, Mary Magdalene and Mary, the Mother of James, went to the tomb with spices to give Jesus a proper burial, but found that the stone had been rolled away and the body of their savior was gone. The women ran to the disciples and told them what they had found. In disbelief, Peter ran to the tomb and saw only the linen cloths in his place.

Later in the text, Jesus appeared to Cleopas and another traveler and broke bread with them and they knew Him. Luke 24:35 says,

> *"Then the two went over everything that happened on the road and how they recognized him when he broke the bread."*[7]

Here in the scripture the word *recognize* means that they perceived that He was the Christ because they spent time together. The Greek translation of the word recognize is ginosko. It means *to include, to learn, to know, to have knowledge of, and to become acquainted with.*[8] The last definition that I want to draw your attention to is *the Jewish idiom for sexual intercourse between a man and a woman.*[9] To lay down the ground work, the sexual intercourse that I am talking about is between a married couple that is holy unto God. So here in the scripture, Cleopas and his traveler are saying that because they spent time together they knew Jesus intimately. That means at some point before Jesus' death, they had to listen to Jesus' sermons. Maybe they were included in the five thousand that were fed on the mountain. Possibly, they saw Jesus heal the leper. So here you have a follower of Jesus Christ, who knew that he was crucified just a few days ago, perceiving that he was indeed the Christ. Furthermore, they recognized him through the breaking of bread, which was Christ's example of relationship building.

Do you know God intimately? Do you have that relationship with Him, wherein you immediately know God's voice? I want to challenge you in the area of prayer. If you are going to be an effective worship leader, you must have a prayer life. There must be evidence of your relationship with Him.

The act of prayer and intercession must become just as vital in the worship experience as singing. Prayer moves the worship experience into the next dimension where the very works of Satan are destroyed by the power of the Almighty God. As a worshipper the truth of the matter is, if you want to see the yoke destroying move of God, you must have a prayer life. If you want to see bodies healed, you must know how to go to the throne room of God. The fact is that worship does not begin on Sunday morning or at your midweek service. Worship begins during your prayer time. It is during your prayer time that you begin to pray for the people of God. It is at that moment that you begin to pray for a mighty move of God's glory. If you want to build *The Dwelling Place* for His presence, then seek His face.

A TRANSFORMED MIND MOVES YOU CLOSER TO HIM

Now, I want to challenge you again. In Romans 12:2, it instructs you to be transformed by the renewing of your mind. If your knowledge of God brings about a change, your mind will have to be included in that transformation. The brain is where your thoughts originate. The brain sends and receives signals throughout the body. It is also, where you process information and make decisions. This is why it is vitally important for you to be transformed in your mind. How can you make wise, godly decisions when your mind is focused on worldly things?

In Chapter One, I shared Romans 12:1-2 with you from the The Message Bible. To impress the importance of this scripture upon you, I must mention it again.

> *"So here's what I want you to do, God helping you: Take your everyday, ordinary life—your sleeping, eating, going-to-work, and walking—around life—and place it before God as an offering. Embracing what God does for you is the best thing you can do for him. Don't become so well-adjusted to your culture that you fit into it without even thinking. Instead, fix your attention on God. You'll be changed from the inside out. Readily recognized what he wants from you, and quickly respond to it. Unlike the culture around you, always dragging you down to its level of immaturity, God brings the best out of you, develops well-formed maturity in you."*[10]

As a worship leader, it is important that you renew your mind. I know that when you usually hear of renewing your mind it is with the Word of God...and I totally agree. Here, I want to take it a little deeper. I want to challenge you to change your thought patterns. I want you to change the way you think. Truthfully, you may not have grown up in a house like the Cosby's, where every problem was resolved in half an hour. You may still carry hurts and pains from years gone by. You may not be able to forgive someone who molested you. You may find it hard to forgive a father who deserted you.

At this very moment, you must make a choice. Are you going to live by the world's standards of holding on to past hurts and pains? Will you say that you will forgive, but not forget? Are you going to fit into this culture's rule that it is all about me and what I can do for myself? Or, are you going to renew your mind and change your thought patterns? This may not be easy. You may have to make a list of these negative and worldly thoughts and then write positive and godly thoughts. When the negative thoughts begin to flood your mind, you will be able to change your thought pattern with positive words. When you make the decision to think in a positive and godly manner, you are renewing your mind. This process must work with the Word of God and with prayer.

The evidence of the Word of God, prayer and a renewed mind is found in the fruit that your life produces. Galatians 5:22-23 says,

> *"But what happens when we live God's way? He brings gifts into our lives, much the same way that fruit appears in an orchard—things like affection for others, exuberance about life, serenity. We develop a willingness to stick with things, a sense of compassion in the heart, and a conviction that a basic holiness permeates things and people. We find ourselves involved in loyal commitments, not needing to force our way in life, able to marshal and direct our energies wisely."*[11]

In this scripture, you can see the practicality of living a holy lifestyle. The conclusion is that it affects your character, making you a better person. Your goal as a worshipper should be to build a dwelling place for God whereby the people of God will be able to enter into His presence. There is a grave responsibility that is placed upon you. I pray that you will understand that the role of a worship leader is more than just singing. Your lifestyle must testify of your knowledge of God through your transformation into His likeness. Therefore, it will be through your knowledge of Him, that you will be able to worship Him.

ENDNOTES

1. Worship, The Church on the Threshold page, http://www.monergism.com/thethreshold/articles/topic/worship.html.
2. New Living Translation.
3. King James Version
4. The Message Bible.
5. Psalm 104:1 King James Version.
6. The Message Bible.
7. The Message Bible.
8. The Book of Luke Chapter 24. Heartlight's Search God's Word page. http://www.searchgodsword.org/isb/bible.cgi?query=lu+24%3A30§ion=0&it=nas&oq=lu%252024%3A30&ot=bhs&nt=na&new=1&nb=lu&ng=24&nlc=%A0%A0%3E%7C%A0%A0&ncc=24
9. The Book of Luke Chapter 24.
10. The Message Bible.

Chapter Five

WHAT DO YOU CALL HIM?

IMAGINE THAT YOU WERE attending a banquet and someone asked you to say a few words about the guest speaker. The only problem is that you have never met the person. No one gave you his biography. You try asking a few people about him, but everyone just points you to someone else. You even tried to Google™ him, but to no avail. Now the time has finally arrived. You get up to the podium and you look at all the faces and say...

WORSHIP IS BIRTHED OUT OF YOUR EXPERIENCE

This is similar to your experience in worship. While the music is hot, you are all in, jumping and thinking about the words of the songs. However, when the music slows from praise to worship and the leader directs you to sing a song unto the Lord, you draw a blank. You wonder what to say and you find yourself echoing the words of the worship leader. Although this is usually the flow into the song of the Lord, as a worship leader you must worship out of your personal relationship and experience with God. What has He done for you? Has he healed you? Did you receive a job without the proper qualifications? Were you able to buy property below market value? Did He heal you of cancer? Or, did a lump miraculously dry up? These are real-life examples of miracles God does daily for His people.

WORSHIP COMES OUT OF YOUR UNDERSTANDING

In Exodus 15, God had just delivered the children of Israel from Pharaoh. The Children of Israel had just seen the miracle of the parting of the Red Sea. They also experienced the miracle of walking on dry land. So here in Exodus 15:1-3, Moses and the children of Israel sang songs unto the Lord.

I will sing to the Lord,
For He has triumphed gloriously!
The horse and its rider
He has been thrown into the sea!
The Lord is my strength and song,
And He has become my salvation;
He is my God, and I will praise Him;
My father's God and I will exalt Him.
The Lord is a man of war;
The Lord is His name.[1]

I believe that the children of Israel sang unto the Lord because they had an understanding of God. The more they praised God, the more He blessed them.

Can you imagine receiving a gift from a friend? When you open the gift, you are disappointed. Although you do not say anything, your face says it all. So you find it within yourself to give an empty thank you. How do you think your friend feels since he spent time picking out the gift? Do you think your friend would be eager to buy you something else? It is likely that your friend will be hesitant to buy you gifts in the future. Just like your friend, God loves praise. He loves to hear your gratitude. He longs to hear the sincerity in your worship. God takes joy in your happiness. When you praise Him, God will continue to bless you.

YOU MUST KNOW HIM BEFORE YOU CAN WORSHIP HIM

How can you show your thankfulness to God if you do not know His character? Before you can build a dwelling place for God, you must know who He is. You must have a personal experience with Him. In Mark 8:26-29, Jesus asks his disciples two questions. The first question: "*Who do men say that I am?*" The second question: "*But who do you say that I am?*" I believe that the questions were used to test the disciples. Jesus already knew what people were saying about him. He was not concerned about what others had to say. He wanted to know what his disciples had to say—the ones who walked with him. He was challenging the disciples. Can you imagine? The disciples had just seen Jesus feed five thousand. They saw Jesus walk on water. They watched as many touched Him and were healed. After witnessing all of these miracles, Jesus questions them. You would think that after such an experience, all of the disciples would have been jumping to answer the second question with their hands waving in the air. Lord, I know...I know the answer! Despite the many miracles they had seen, was that enough to convince them? Witnessing miracles does not mean that you awaken to the knowledge of the Almighty God. So as in the scripture, I am going to place the weight of the second question on you. Who do you say that He is? Will you answer like Peter, or will you sit and contemplate?

As a worshipper, you must know God. You cannot hide behind

the sound board or your position. Each member of the Sanctuary Ministries has a responsibility to be able to articulate the goodness of God. I do not want you to be like the disciples who were not able to answer the question. During worship, I want you to be able to respond to the movement of God with understanding. You must be able to describe God in multiple ways. I have listed the Hebrew names of God to give you a head start in your worship experience. Whenever you are in doubt, you can refer to this book. This list should not be used as a script, but as a springboard. As you continue to grow, I would admonish you to continue to learn about the character and nature of God.

THE HEBREW NAMES OF GOD

EL

God as Mighty, Strong and Prominent. It used 250 times in the Old Testament. See Gen. 7:1, 28:3, 35:11; Nu. 23:22, Josh. 3:10; 2 Sam. 22:31, 32.[2]

ELOHIM

God as Creator, Preserver, Transcendent, Mighty and Strong. It occurs 2,570 times in the Old Testament. See Gen. 17:7, 6:18, 9:15, 50:24, 1 Kings 8:23; Jer. 31:33; Isa. 40:1, Isa. 54:5, 1 Sam. 45:18.[3]

EL SHADDAI

God Almighty or God all Sufficient. It is used 48 times in the Old Testament. See Gen. 31:29, 49:24, 25; Prov. 3:27; Micah 2:1; Isa. 60:15, 16; Isa. 66:1-13, Ruth 1:20, 21.[4]

ADONAI

Master or Lord. It is used 300 times in the Old Testament. See Gen.

15:2, Ex. 4:10, Judges 6:15, 2 Sam. 7:18-20, Ps. 8, Ps. 114:7; Ps. 135:5, Ps. 141:8, Ps. 109:21-28.[5]

JEHOVAH

The name of God. Yahweh is the covenant name of God. It occurs 6823 times in the Old Testament. It comes from the verb "to be", havah. It refers to the Self-Existent One, "I AM WHO I AM" or "I WILL BE WHO I WILL BE' as revealed to Moses at the burning bush (Ex 3). See Gen. 2:4; Dan. 9:14; Ps. 11:7; Lev. 19:2; Hab. 1:12.[6]

JEHOVAH-JIREH

The Lord will provide. Gen 22:12. It comes from the root "jireh" which means to provide or to foresee as a prophet.[7]

JEHOVAH-ROPHE

The Lord who heals. Ex. 15:22-26. It comes from the root "rophe" which means to heal. It implies spiritual, emotional as well as physical healing. See Jer. 30:17, 3:22, Isa. 61:1. God heals body, soul; and spirit; all levels of man's being.[8]

JEHOVAH-NISSI

The Lord our banner. Ex. 17:15. God on the battlefield. It comes from the word which means "to glisten" and "to lift up".[9]

JEHOVAH-M'KADDESH

The Lord who sanctifies. Lev. 20:8. It means to make whole, set apart for holiness.[10]

JEHOVAH-SHALOM

The Lord of peace. Judges 6:24. The word Shalom is translated into the word peace. It was also used 170 times in the Bible and means whole, finished, fulfilled, and perfected. It is also related to the words well and welfare. See Deut. 27:6; Dan. 5:26; 1 Kings 9:25, 1 Kings 8:61; Gen. 15:16; Ex. 21:34; Ex. 22:5, 6; Lev. 7:11-21. Shalom means that kind of peace that results from being a whole person in right relationship to God and to one's fellow man.[11]

SHEPHERD

Ps. 23; Ps. 79:13; Ps. 95:7; Ps. 80:1; Ps. 100:3; Gen. 49:24; Isa. 40:11.[12]

JUDGE

Ps. 7:8, 96:13.[13]

JEHOVAH ELOHIM

The Lord God Gen 2:4; Judges 5:3; Isa. 17:6, Zeph. 2:9; Ps. 59:5.[14]

JEHOVAH-TSIDKENU

The Lord our righteousness. Jer. 23:5, 6; Jer. 6, Jer. 33:16.[15]

JEHOVAH-ROHI

The Lord our shepherd. Ps. 23.[16]

JEHOVAH-SHAMMAH

The Lord is there. Ezek. 48:35.[17]

JEHOVAH-SABAOTH

The Lord of Hosts. The commander of the angelic host and the armies of God. Isa. 1:24; Ps. 46:7, 11; 2 Kings 3:9-12; Jer. 11:20, Rom. 9:29; James 5:4; Rev. 19: 11-16.[18]

EL ELYON

Most High. Deut. 26:19, 32:8; Ps. 18:13; Gen. 14:18; Nu. 24:16; Ps. 78:35, 7:17, 18:13, 97:9, 66:2, 7:56, 18:13; Dan. 7:25, 27; Is 14:14.[19]

ABHIR

Mighty One or to be strong. Gen. 49:24; Deut. 10:17; Ps. 132:2, 5 Isa. 1:24, 49:26, 60:1.[20]

KADOSH

Holy One. Isaiah uses the expression "the Holy One of Israel" 29 times. Ps. 71:22; Isa. 40:25, 43:3, 48:17.[21]

SHAPHAT

Judge. Gen. 18:25.[22]

EL ROI

God of Seeing or the one who open our eyes. Gen. 16:13.[23]

KANA

Jealous or zealous. Ex. 20:5, 34:14; Deut. 5:9; Isa. 9:7; Zech. 1:14, 8:2.[24]

PALET

Deliverer. Ps. 18:2.[25]

YESHA

Savior. Isa. 43:3. Jesus is the Greek equivalent of the Hebrew "Joshua." The latter is a contraction of Je-Hoshua. (Christ, the anointed one is equivalent to the Hebrew Maschiah, or Messiah).[26]

GAOL

Redeemer or to buy back by paying a price. Job 19:25.[27]

MAGEN

Shield. Ps. 3:3, 18:30.[28]

EYALUTH

Strength. Ps. 22:19.[29]

TSADDIQ

Righteous One. Ps. 22:19.[30]

EL-OLAM

Everlasting God or God of everlasting time. Gen. 21:33; Ps. 90:1-3, 93:2; Isa. 26:4.[31]

EL-BERITH

God of the Covenant. Judges 9:46. This word was probably originally used to refer to the God of Israel.[32]

EL-GIBHOR

Mighty God. Isa. 9:6.[33]

ZUR

God of our rock. Deut. 32:18; Isa. 30:29.[34]

ATTQ YOMIN (ARAMAIC)

Ancient of Days, Dan. 7:9, 13, 22.[35]

MELEKH

King Ps. 5:2, 29:10, 44:4, 47:6-8, 48:2, 68:24, 74:12, 95:3, 97:1, 99:4, 146:10, Isa. 5:1, 5, 41:21, 43:15, 44:6, 52:7, 52:10.[36]

Use this information as a foundation in worship. Now when the worship leader directs you to sing a song unto the Lord, you can say that He is a banner over you. You can say that he is your strength. He is your rock, Mighty God and King. Furthermore, the more you know of Him, the greater the revelation of Him.

ENDNOTES

1. New King James Version.
2. Old Testament (The Hebrew Scriptures, or Tanach). The Names of God page by Lambert Dolphin. http://www.ldolphin.org/names/html.

3-36. Old Testament (The Hebrew Scriptures, or Tanach).

Chapter Six

ENTER THE GLORY

Have you ever attended an elementary school concert? As the band begins to warm up all of the sounds and rhythms are struggling to fit together as they attempt to create a melody. It is almost as if you can hear the clashing symbols, the squeaky violin and the thunderous trombone—as each musician, attempts to create the sound, that particular sound that would bring a smile to his parent's face. Although it may not be the Philharmonic, each parent sits proudly while he or she listens to his little star.

Now can you imagine God sitting in heaven watching as each service begins, like those parents at the elementary school concert? The praise team, musicians and dancers are preparing to minister. Each team comes together to use its gifts to the glory of God. If everyone was perfect and lived perfect lives this would be simple. However, the truth of the matter is that everyone is dealing with something. Someone may have just lost a job, while another may have lost a loved one. Someone else was just stuck in traffic, while another just had a disagreement with his spouse and, now, it is time for the service to begin. It is time to create the place for the glory of the Lord to dwell among the corporate body. However, how can the glory of God dwell among His people when the focus is elsewhere?

This is not to say that what you are going through is not important. I believe the preliminaries of checking the microphones and the sound, amidst all of our personal issues or should I say distractions, becomes like that clashing sound at the beginning of that elementary school concert. Everyone is trying to fit his life, attitude, and mind-set into worship. However, the corporate body cannot enter worship with all of this clanging noise hindering the move of God.

YOU MUST CREATE AN ATMOSPHERE WHERE HIS PRESENCE CAN DWELL

So how do you move into to the place where the spirit of the Lord can dwell among the corporate body of believers? 2 Chronicles 5:13 says:

> *"And when the trumpeters and singers were joined in unison, making one sound to be heard in praising and thanking the Lord, and when they lifted up their voice with the trumpets and cymbals and other instruments for song and praised the Lord, saying, For He is good, for His mercy and loving-kindness endure forever, then the house of the Lord was filled with a cloud, So that the priests could not stand to minister because of the cloud, for the glory of the Lord filled the house of God."*[1]

Every Sunday morning I meet with the praise team, musicians, media and choir. I encourage them to go forth in worship. Although everyone may have had issues before arriving to church, I expect each person to move beyond his or her personal hang-ups because it is time to enter the glory of the Lord. I explained that everyone has a responsibility to the people of God because someone is looking for a miracle and everyone must create the atmosphere for the spirit of the Lord to dwell. In the scripture, it said that *when the trumpeters and singers were joined together in unison, making one sound...the glory of the Lord filled the house*. I believe that this is more than knowing how to harmonize and flow together. I believe that when everyone comes together with the mindset to create one sound, and use their gifts and talents unto the glory of God, that He will show up. As a worship leader, you must move beyond your personal issues. You have a great responsibility as a Levite to create one sound.

YOU MUST FOLLOW THE PATTERN

This is why the pattern of building a dwelling place for His presence is so important. By this time, you should have worked on yourself, understood your place as a worship leader, and obtained an understanding of the flow of worship. Right now, you have the responsibility of leading the people of God. I share with my worship team all the time that you have to go in and get what you need quickly because someone is depending upon your praise. Someone is looking for you to worship God in a way that makes them believe that cancer can dry up or that the lame can walk.

YOU MUST WORK TO CREATE ONE SOUND IN WORSHIP

Oh, how I pray for the day that every worship leader would get to the place where he understands the importance of uniting to create one sound unto the glory of God. I pray that every member of the Sanctuary Ministries would learn to work together, pray together, and bring every gift together for the sole purpose of creating this one sound. When the holy sound is made in the earth, you will see the glory of God show up. I am not talking about His glory that makes you feel good or that makes you feel accepted in Him. However, I am looking for His glory that brings signs, wonders and miracles.

I really want you to see how serious your position is when it comes to healing and deliverance. Through the glory of God, you will see deliverance from drugs and alcohol. When the glory of God shows up, I believe that it will save someone's marriage that is on the verge of divorce. The glory of the Lord brings a manifestation to the corporate body for the purpose of healing, deliverance, sanctification, and justification. It will be at this moment that the glory of the Lord can fill the house. The corporate body will experience the fullness of His glory when everyone understands the unity of praise.

THE GLORY OF THE LORD BRINGS WEALTH

In Hebrew, the word glory means, *abundance, riches, wealth, splendor, dignity, honor, and reputation*. When you ask for the glory of the Lord to come and dwell among the corporate body, you are asking for abundance, riches and wealth. This is why Matthew 6:33 says to seek the kingdom of heaven first and his righteousness, and all these things will be added unto you. In the Message Bible it reads:

> *"If God gives such attention to the appearance of wild flowers-most of which are never seen-don't you think he'll attend to you, take pride in you, do his best for you? What I'm trying to do here is to get you to relax, to not be so preoccupied with getting, so you can respond to God's giving. People who don't know God and his works fuss over these things, but you know both God and how he works. Steep your life in God-reality, God initiative, God provisions. Don't worry about missing out. You'll find all your everyday human concerns met".*[2]

In the scripture, Jesus is teaching and says, *"Relax!"* You don't have to worry about your everyday needs. When you put God first, everything will be provided for you. If God cares for the appearance of wild flowers and most of them are on the side of the road and are never seen, can you imagine how much God cares for you? You must begin to change your focus from self-focus to God-focus because everything that you need is found in His glory.

As you begin the process of entering the glory of the Lord, you must understand His glory.

THE GLORY OF THE LORD IS GREAT

In Psalms 138:5, the glory of the Lord is described as great. It reads:

> *"Yes, they shall sing of the ways of the Lord and joyfully celebrate His mighty acts, for great is the glory of the Lord."*[3]

So here in the scripture, it shows the greatness of our God. Since His glory is great, it brings about mighty acts and deeds. Therefore, you can find miracles, signs and wonders in His glory. Israel understood the glory of the Lord because they experienced it personally. They experienced His glory at the crossing of the Red Sea. They experienced it through the manna from heaven. God showed forth His presence to them in so many ways. Psalm 113:4-5 says, *"The Lord is high above the heavens, who is like unto the Lord our God, who dwelleth on high".*[4] At that moment in the scripture, there was a revelation that nothing was, is or ever shall be greater than God. Also in Psalm 104:32, it describes the greatness of God by saying, *"Who looks on the earth, and it quakes and trembles, Who touches the mountains, and they smoke!"*[5]

God's glory is so great that He can cause earthquakes and volcanoes. Can you imagine what would happen when every worship leader entered worship expecting to see the greatness of God's glory? Can you imagine what would happen if each member of the Sanctuary Ministries started each service with the expectation of seeing miracles? I anticipate the day when the corporate body of believers will experience the presence of His glory in a way that shows forth His might and power. Someone will just walk into the presence of God and growths will fall off instantaneously. Deaf ears will pop open and will hear because you worshipped with the expectation of His greatness.

GOD'S GREATNESS SUPERSEDES YOUR IMAGINATION

The expectation that I am talking about goes beyond your imagination. If you can think of His greatness, than it is not God. God's greatness exceeds your mere imagination and takes you to where He is. It is in the greatness of His glory that you take on His mindset—a holy mindset. At this moment in worship, you will experience a mighty move of His glory in magnitudes and numbers that you have never experienced before.

I want to delve a little deeper and describe the greatness of God. One of the most devastating natural disasters was the Tsunami in South Asia. I did a little research on the Tsunami that literally blew my mind.

"The tsunami is caused by a submarine earthquake, by an underwater or coastal landslide, or by the eruption of a volcano. After the earthquake or other generating impulse occurs, a train of simple, progressive oscillatory waves is propagated great distances over the

ocean surface in ever-widening circles, much like waves produced by a pebble falling into a shallow pool. In deep water a tsunami can travel as fast 500 miles per hour. The wavelengths are enormous, about 60 to 120 miles. The effects of these waves are so great that it can uproot trees, pull buildings from their foundations, carry boats far inshore, and wash away beaches."[6]

Can you imagine what will happen when each worship leader understands the greatness of God's glory in relation to the greatness shown in the effects of a tsunami? Can you imagine blind eyes opening after being in darkness for 30 years? Can you imagine the mighty wave of God's glory resting upon homes and churches? Can you imagine the effects of God's glory sweeping nations? Can you begin to imagine the effects of His presence? Can you imagine creating a sound in worship that awakens the glory of the Lord in such a way that it uproots habits and hobbies? Can you see the wave of His glory as it changes lives, heals the sick, and set the captives free? It is time that you move from the mechanical, business as usual worship service and move into the God expecting worship service.

THE GLORY OF THE LORD IS ETERNAL

In Psalms 104:31, the glory of God is described as eternal. It reads:

"The glory of the Lord shall endure for ever; the Lord shall rejoice in His works."[7]

Since the glory of the Lord is eternal, then I can only conclude that His glory is never changing. His glory remains the same from age to age. This is why you cannot put glory in man. You cannot glory in your own works, because your glory will fade. How many times have you seen an athlete return after retirement? Most often, due to age, condition of the body and mental state, the athlete should have stayed in retirement because his glory days have ended.

God's glory, on the other hand, never changes. He is always the same. Matthew 24:35 says, *"Heaven and earth shall pass away, but my words shall not pass away."*[8] So here, when I begin to talk about the eternal nature of God's glory, it becomes a challenge for you in the area of your faith. A worship leader may have faith in his gifts and talents. He may believe that it is because he has a beautiful voice that the glory of the Lord visits the service. He may put faith in his title, believing that it is because he is the musical director that causes the glory of the Lord to visit the service. He may put glory in his role as an usher because he controls the seating of the service. However, God does not need you to be glorious. God's glory existed when He made the heavens and the earth. God's glory existed when He formed Adam from the dust of the ground and brought the sea into existence. As a worship leader, you show forth His glory through your praise. Psalms 50:23 says, *"He who brings an offering of praise and thanksgiving honors and glorifies Me."*[9]

Everyone has seen the movie, *The Wizard of Oz*. In the movie, Dorothy is trying to get back home. Along her journey, she met the tin man who needed a heart, a cowardly lion who wanted courage and a scarecrow who wanted a brain. Amidst the adversity of the wicked witch of the west, and the tests given to them by the Wizard of Oz, Dorothy and her friends were able to succeed until they found out that the wizard was just a man. Not only did she find out that the wizard was just a man, but she also found that the whole ordeal was just a dream.

YOU MUST BELIEVE IN THE ETERNAL NATURE OF GOD

The eternal nature of God will cause you to believe that He is real and that He will reign forever. Unlike Dorothy, you do not have to worry about awaking one morning and finding that God was just a dream. He has given you His Word. He has given signs, wonders and miracles that show forth His power. You cannot allow your praise experience to be in vain because, like Dorothy, you are performing all of these deeds just for a man.

God is greater than any thing, and that includes any one. He is greater than any position. You must realize that when you go into the presence of the Almighty God that it is not about you trying to make an impression. It is about paying homage to the one and only God, in all of His glory. You can search the world and find no one like Him. For His love is eternal. His peace is eternal. His loving kindness endures forever. His glory reaches beyond your finite mind and into infinity. You worship Him because He is God.

THE GLORY OF THE LORD IS RICH

In Ephesians 3:16, the glory of the Lord is described as rich. It reads,

> *"May He grant you out of the rich treasury of His glory to be strengthened and reinforced with mighty power in the inner man by the [Holy] Spirit [Himself indwelling your innermost being and personality]."*[10]

In Ephesians 3, Paul wrote to the saints in Ephesus. In this chapter, he is encouraging them to not faint at the sight of tribulation, but to be strengthened by the richness of His glory in the inner man. I know that everyone is looking for wealth and there is nothing wrong with that. However, before God can trust you with the riches and the wealth, He must first know that you are prepared in your inner man. The truth of the matter is that everything that you need is found in the glory of God, and that includes riches.

When I began to meditate on the word rich, I began to think of ice cream and cake that are sometimes referred to as rich. Many times when either ice cream or cake is too rich, you may choose to shy away from eating too much because you do not want to become sick. When I think of the word rich, I also think of luxury. There is nothing like walking into a luxury car dealership, hotel, or store. The quality of the product and the customer service is held at a higher standard. So comparing that to the richness of God's glory, there must be some distinct features that make the glory of the Lord rich.

If you look at Ephesians 3:17-18 it reads,

"That Christ may dwell in your hearts by faith; that ye, being rooted and grounded in love, May be able to comprehend with all saints what is the breadth, and length, and depth and height; And to know the love of Christ, which passeth knowledge, that ye might be filled with all the fullness of God."[11]

In the scripture, it shows that if you are going to receive the rich treasures of His glory, you must first be rooted and grounded in love. Through love, you will understand the breadth and length, depth and height of God. The greatest of all riches that you can have is love. Mark 8:36 says, *"What good would it do to get everything you want and lose you, the real you? What could you ever trade your soul for?"*[12]

If you are going to experience the true riches of His glory, you must first love your neighbor. As a worship leader and a member of the Sanctuary Ministries, you must be the first to forgive. You must be the first to let go, because you cannot allow anything to hinder the move of God's glory and prevent the people of God from experiencing the richness of His glory. The great thing about the word rich is that it can mean something different to different people at different times.

YOU MUST LIVE WORTHY OF THE RICHNESS OF HIS GLORY

As a worship leader, you must live in a way that allows the richness of God's glory to enter the worship experience so that everyone's needs are supplied. It is important that you do not block someone's blessing because of what you have in your heart. I share with my praise team all the time that they must ask for forgiveness before worship because what is in their hearts could hinder the move of God's glory. Each member of the Sanctuary Ministries, must show forth the richness of God.

When it comes to the worship experience, the worship team must create the connection for the congregation with the power source, who is Jesus Christ. The congregation should not be aware of your gifts or abilities to sing a high note. They should connect to the burden removing and yoke destroying richness of God that causes them to enter into His presence in a very special and unique way. It is my prayer that the corporate body will experience a very special and unique anointing from God.

Once you experience the richness of His glory through love,

Ephesians 3:20 says that He will do *"exceeding abundantly above all that we ask or think according to the power that worketh within us."*[13] How I long for the day that you will experience the full riches of God's glory in every church service and in your life. It will be at that moment that you will see the true manifestation of God in your life. I believe that it will catapult you into an arena that is far beyond your understanding, for the riches of God are unsearchable.

You cannot begin to imagine the great things that God has in store for you. Once you experience the richness of His glory, God is going to enrich your experience with Him. It is not going to be business as usual, but you will worship with purpose and understanding. Out of that experience, you are going to become wealthy, beyond your imagination, in every area of your life. Everything about you is going to become luxurious because you are representative of the King. Your family is going to become luxurious and be an example to the world. Your marriage is going to be wealthy with peace and understanding. Your children are going to be rich with knowledge and understanding. And yes, even far beyond your imagination, God is going to do even greater exploits in your life.

TRUE WORSHIP IS ABOUT GOD

Worship is not about looking to see what God can do for you. It is about expressing how you feel about Him amidst your struggles and pain, knowing that He will come through. When you worship God, you will see life from His perspective. It will allow you to move from where you are and to see from a kingly perspective.

In worship, you exalt the name of the Lord with a new song, in the dance, and with our mouths. Psalm 149 says,

"PRAISE THE Lord! Sing to the Lord a new song, praise Him in the assembly of His saints! Let Israel rejoice in Him, their Maker; let Zion's children triumph and be joyful in their King!
Let them praise His name in chorus and choir and with the [single or group] dance; let them sing praises to Him with the tambourine and lyre!
For the Lord takes pleasure in His people; He will beautify the humble with salvation and adorn the wretched with victory.
Let the saints be joyful in the glory and beauty [which God confers upon them]; let them sing for joy upon their beds.
Let the high praises of God be in their throats and a two-edged sword in their hands,
To wreak vengeance upon the nations and chastisements upon the peoples,
To bind their kings with chains, and their nobles with fetters of iron,
To execute upon them the judgment written. He [the Lord] is the honor of all His saints. Praise the Lord! (Hallelujah!)[14]

In the scripture, it addresses each area in which you can exalt the glory of the Lord. The first way you can exalt the Lord is with your voice. You are instructed to sing a new song unto the Lord. The worship team is responsible for teaching new songs to the congregation. The song choice is very important to the worship experience because it sets the stage for the rest of the service. As a side bar, it is important that you consult with your Pastor to see what he is teaching so that your song choice will be in line with the Word of God. There is no particular formula for the song choice. In my church, the Abundant Life Family Worship Church, the worship team sings two praise songs with one worship song. However, I explained to the worship leaders that if one song takes us into the throne room of God, to leave it there. It is important to remain flexible to the move of the Holy Spirit. It can never be about your agenda. It is always about God's agenda.

In the scripture that talks about a *new song*, I believe that this is where the worship team and the musicians move into the prophetic. The song of the Lord is manifested when you create a dwelling place in you for His presence to be dominant. In John 10:27, it says, *"My sheep recognize my voice. I know them and they follow me."*[15] When you hear His voice, you can only obey His voice. When you hear the song of the Lord, you no longer hear the song that you have on paper. You literally begin to write new songs.

YOU CONNECT WITH GOD THROUGH THE SPIRIT

It is through the Spirit that you connect with the Lord and begin to sing. I believe that many songs have yet to be written because they were sung and not recorded during this time. I also believe that the song of the Lord moves into the prophetic. When the worship team and the musicians begin to move into the prophetic, they become the voice of God. They begin to speak as God would speak to the people of God. It becomes a word from the Lord in the atmosphere of music.

This is the time where the worship experience moves from just offering up the praises to God and into the glory dwelling with the corporate body. It is at this moment that God's glory is revealed and the worship moves into a supernatural experience and expression of God. The worship team experiences the glory and gives off an expression to the people of God. For example, the worship leader may experience the glory of the Lord and say, "For the Lord is great and mighty" and then instructs the people to follow in song. It is through this expression of God that the congregation is able to experience the glory of the Lord. I am not talking about a spooky experience, but a God experience.

In Ephesians 6:12 says,

> *"For we are not wrestling with flesh and blood [contending only with physical opponents], but against the despotisms, against the powers, against [the master spirits who are] the world rulers of this present darkness, against the spirit forces of wickedness in the heavenly (supernatural) sphere."*[16]

Once you enter the arena of the new song, you are waging war through song. If someone is looking to be healed from HIV, it is not going to come because you simply sang a song unto the Lord. God is going to heal because you understood that you were coming against every demonic spirit that is tied into HIV. When you sing a new song unto the Lord, angels are dispatched to wage war. This war is not against an opponent that you can see. This war is against spiritual forces in high places.

Are you ready? Are you in the place to hear from God? Can you hear the sound of God? Can you hear the approach of His glory? As a worshipper, you must be prepared at all times because God's glory is highly exalted through the song. It is through the sound, the heavenly sound, that God's name is exalted above the heavens and the earth.

THE GLORY OF THE LORD IS EXALTED IN THE DANCE

The glory of the Lord is also exalted in the dance. 2 Sam 6:14 says,

> *"And David danced before the Lord with all his might, clad in a linen ephod [a priest's upper garment]."*[17]

In this chapter, David was transporting the ark of the Covenant. While they were transporting the ark, the ark stumbled and Uzzah tried to catch it with his hand. The Lord killed Uzzah because it was forbidden to touch the ark. In his haste to catch the ark, Uzzah lost his reverence and fear for the glory of God. Not only did Uzzah make a deadly mistake, Israel was also guilty because they carried the ark in a cart instead of on the Levites' shoulders.

As a result of Uzzah's death, David became afraid. Obed-edom, a Levite, offered to take the ark of the covenant. Obed-edom and his family knew how to reverence the ark of God and his whole household was blessed. After three months had passed, David heard of the blessings that were upon Obed-edom's house and brought the ark into the city of David with gladness. It was at this moment that David danced before the Lord with all of his might.

Personally, I am sure that God could have killed everyone. However, he took only Uzzah as an example. I am sure David was afraid of the consequences because he did not want to bring the ark to the city of David. When David realized the mercies of God, he could only show his joy for God's unmerited favor. So, in the scripture it says that he danced before the Lord. David's dance was not a usual dance.

He danced until the glory of the Lord was revealed. He did not care about who was looking. He did not care if anyone else was dancing with him. He danced because he understood that there had to be an expression of joy towards God. As a worship leader, you must not limit your worship experience to just singing. You must express praise to God in a dance, for God delights in seeing his people joyous.

THE GLORY OF THE LORD IS EXALTED WITH YOUR MOUTH

The glory of the Lord is also exalted through your mouth. If you look back at Psalms 149:6-7, it says,

> *"Let the high praises of God be in their throats and a two-edge sword in their hands, to wreak vengeance upon the nations and chastisement upon the peoples."*[18]

In this scripture, you can see that the high praises that come out of your mouth become a weapon of mass destruction against the enemy. I just want to put out any fires. The vengeance that is placed upon the nations and the people, in the scripture, does not come from you. Vengeance belongs only to God.

In Proverbs 18:21, it says, *"Death and life are in the power of the tongue."*[19] In the Message Bible, it says, *"Words kill, words give life; they're either poison or fruit—you choose."*[20] The truth is that what you say matters. If you look back at Psalm 149:6-7, you will see that God uses your words to show forth His glory in the earth. If you want to see your child saved, just began to praise Him. If you want healing in your body, exalt His name. As a worship leader, if you want to see a mighty move of God's glory in the lives of His people, you must begin to worship Him with your mouth.

There will come a time in the worship service where the music will stop. The congregation will begin to cry out to God in worship and adoration. All of the voices will create the sound for the glory of the Lord to be exalted. It will be through your voice that God is going to make changes in the nation. It is through the sound that God is going to reach those unsaved loved ones. When you use the Word of the Lord in worship, God is going to bring forth a mighty deliverance. Zechariah 4:6 says, *"Not by might, nor by power, but by my spirit, saith the Lord of hosts."* This type of deliverance is not going to come simply because you asked for it. It is going to come when you understand the power in the glory of God as it is manifested upon the earth. You are going to experience a mighty move of God through His spirit. So shout aloud. Cry unto God with the voice of triumph!

ENDNOTES

1. King James Version.
2. The Message Bible.
3. King James Version.
4. King James Version.
5. Amplified Bible.
6. Endnote: Tsunami page. Encyclopedia Britannica online. http://www.britannica.com/eb/article-9073633
7. King James Version.
8. King James Version.
9. Amplified Bible.
10. Amplified Bible.
11. King James Version.
12. The Message Bible.
13. King James Version.

14. Amplified Bible.
15. The Message Bible.
16. Amplified Bible.
17. Amplified Bible.
18. Amplified Bible.
19. King James Version.
20. The Message Bible.

Chapter Seven

The Dwelling Place is Within

IT IS MY PRAYER that you understand the purpose of the worship experience. The purpose of the worship experience is to build a dwelling place that is acceptable to the Lord. Through His acceptance, you will see great miracles. In the manifestation of His presence, the corporate body will experience a great deliverance! This dwelling place experience will then move beyond the four walls of the church and into the world.

In 1 Kings 8:10-11 it says,

"When the priests left the Holy Place, a cloud filled The Temple of God. The priests couldn't carry out their priestly duties because of the cloud—the glory of God filled the Temple of God! Then Solomon spoke: God has told us that he lives in the dark where no one can see him; I've built this splendid Temple, O God, to mark your invisible presence forever."[1]

YOUR TEMPLE IS EMPTY WITHOUT THE GLORY OF THE LORD

In the scripture, the temple was just completed but the ark was not placed in it. Although the temple wad designed beautifully, without the ark in the temple, the building was empty. So here in verses 10 and 11, once the ark was in its place the glory of the Lord filled the temple as a sign that He accepted the temple and all of its beauty. If you look back at the scripture, you will see that Solomon created the temple or *The Dwelling Place* to mark God's presence forever! Oh, how I long for the day when the corporate body will see the manifestation of God's approval in each service. I long to see the Almighty God take residence and live within you and experienced throughout the world. 1 Corinthians 6:19 says,

> *"Do you not know that your body is the temple (the very sanctuary) of the Holy Spirit Who lives within you, Whom you have received [as a Gift] from God? You are not your own."*[2]

GOD DESIRES TO DWELL WITHIN YOU

Your body is the temple of the Holy Ghost. This lets you know that God desires to dwell within you. He desires to take residence in you. God wants to set up a place for His glory to dwell. It will be through this experience of His glory where the miraculous will take place. It will be through this glory experience that you will see thousands of people drawn to Him. The corporate body of believers will experience this manifestation because you have taken the time to build a dwelling place that is acceptable unto Him.

THE GLORY OF THE LORD IS NOT JUST FOR YOU

It is my desire that you truly understand that the glory of the Lord is not just for you and the corporate experience. The glory of the Lord should go out into all the land through your life. It is through you that sinners will see the glory of the Lord. It is through the glory of the Lord that is dwelling within you that draws people toward Christ.

In Exodus 40:34-36 it says,

> *"Then the cloud covered the Tabernacle, and the glory of the Lord filled the Tabernacle. Moses could no longer enter the Tabernacle because the cloud had settled down over it, and the glory of the Lord filled the Tabernacle. Now whenever the cloud lifted from the Tabernacle, the people of Israel would set out on their journey, following it."*[3]

I pray that you will take this word and use it in every area of your life. I pray that when you leave the church and go to your home, job or school that you will live worthy of the glory. When you build a dwelling place for God, it is going to affect every area of your life. Take it with you. Live holy and acceptable unto God. When you allow the Holy Presence of God to become the owner of your life you will see wonders and miracles.

Finally, I pray that you will build a dwelling place for His presence so that you can experience all that God has for you, and then take it to the world!

Whether you are a member of the worship team, choir, musicians, ushers, dancers, greeters, media or security become The Dwelling Place for His Presence!

ENDNOTES

1. The Message Bible.
2. Amplified Bible.
3. New Living Translation.

Interested in having a

Praise and Worship Summit at your church?

For more information, please contact:

Abundant Life Family Worship Church

259 George Street

New Brunswick, NJ 08901

Telephone: 732-545-3897

Facsimile: 732-545-2274

www.alfwc.org

NOTES

NOTES

Notes

Notes

Notes

Notes

NOTES

Notes

Notes

Notes

NOTES

Notes